SPACE EXPLORERS
SPACE STATIONS

by Jenny Fretland VanVoorst

po**go**

Ideas for Parents and Teachers

Pogo Books let children practice reading informational text while introducing them to nonfiction features such as headings, labels, sidebars, maps, and diagrams, as well as a table of contents, glossary, and index.

Carefully leveled text with a strong photo match offers early fluent readers the support they need to succeed.

Before Reading

- "Walk" through the book and point out the various nonfiction features. Ask the student what purpose each feature serves.
- Look at the glossary together. Read and discuss the words.

Read the Book

- Have the child read the book independently.
- Invite him or her to list questions that arise from reading.

After Reading

- Discuss the child's questions. Talk about how he or she might find answers to those questions.
- Prompt the child to think more. Ask: Have you ever seen the International Space Station travel through the night sky?

Pogo Books are published by Jump!
5357 Penn Avenue South
Minneapolis, MN 55419
www.jumplibrary.com

Library of Congress Cataloging-in-Publication Data

Names: Fretland VanVoorst, Jenny, 1972- author.
Title: Space stations / by Jenny Fretland VanVoorst.
Description: Minneapolis, MN: Jump!, Inc. [2017]
Series: Space explorers | Audience: Ages 7-10.
Includes bibliographical references and index.
Identifiers: LCCN 2016022245 (print)
LCCN 2016022781 (ebook)
ISBN 9781620314135 (hardcover: alk. paper)
ISBN 9781624964602 (ebook)
Subjects: LCSH: International Space Station—Juvenile literature. | Space Stations—Juvenile literature. Outer space—Exploration—Juvenile literature.
Classification: LCC TL797.15 .F74 2017 (print)
LCC TL797.15 (ebook) | DDC 629.44/2—dc23
LC record available at https://lccn.loc.gov/2016022245

Editor: Kirsten Chang
Series Designer: Anna Peterson
Book Designer: Leah Sanders
Photo Researchers: Kirsten Chang and Leah Sanders

Photo Credits: All photos by Shutterstock except: Alamy, 6-7, 10, 12-13, 18-19; Galyamin Sergej/Shutterstock.com, 14r; Getty, 5, 11; Grisha Bruev/Shutterstock.com, 14l; Superstock, cover, 16-17; Thinkstock, 1, 8-9.

Printed in the United States of America at Corporate Graphics in North Mankato, Minnesota.

TABLE OF CONTENTS

CHAPTER 1

....

WHAT IS A
SPACE STATION?

Have you seen a bright light speeding through the night sky? It might have been a plane. It might have been a shooting star. It might even have been a **satellite**.

But if you're lucky, you may have seen a space station!

Space stations are places where people live and work in space.

They **orbit** Earth. They travel 200 to 300 miles (322 to 483 kilometers) above the planet.

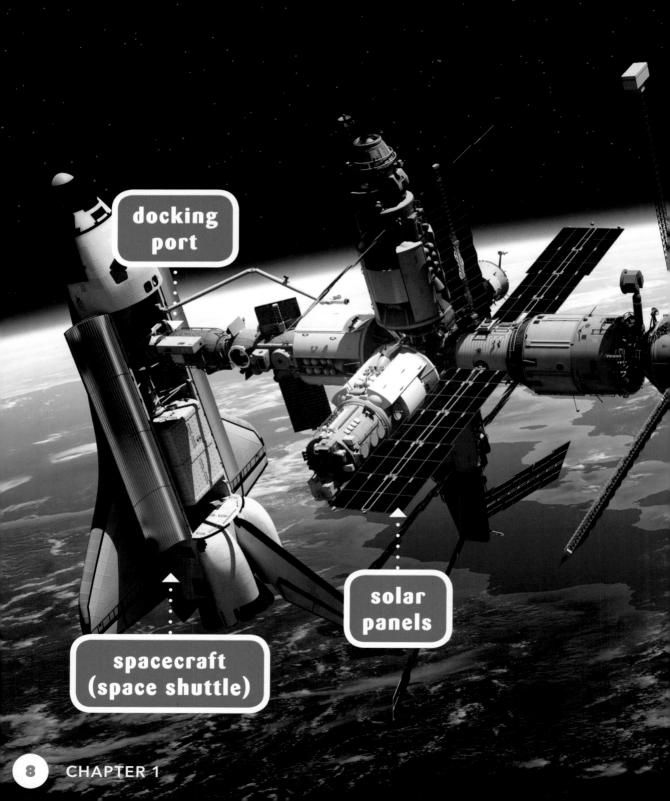

docking
port

spacecraft
(space shuttle)

solar
panels

Space stations have **solar panels**. The panels provide power. They turn sunlight into electricity.

Spacecraft dock with space stations. They bring people. They deliver supplies. All space stations have at least one **docking port**.

CHAPTER 2

··

AT WORK
IN SPACE

Space stations have areas where crews eat, sleep, and exercise. They have areas for work, too.

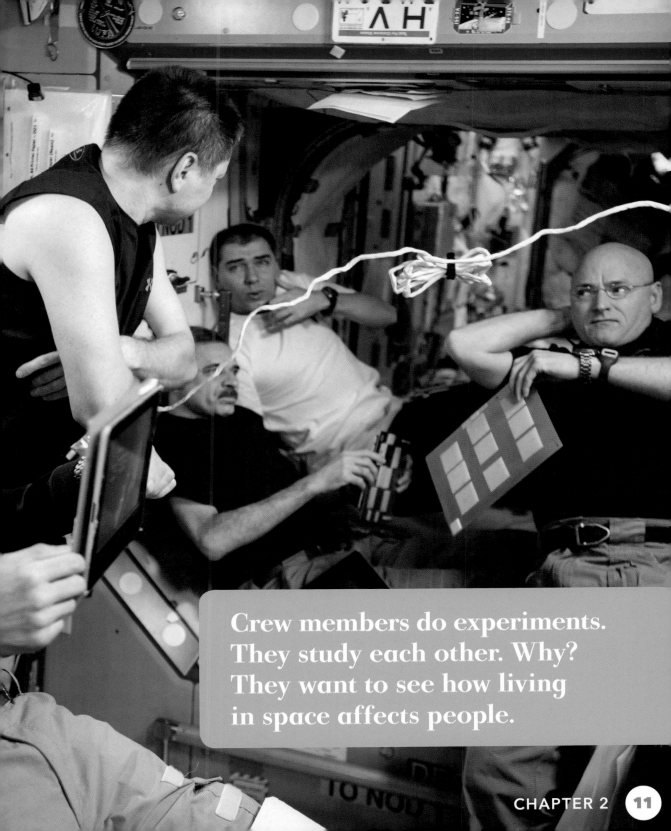

Crew members do experiments. They study each other. Why? They want to see how living in space affects people.

Crews study planets and stars. They study Earth, too. They look for changes over time.

CHAPTER 3

MEET THE
SPACE STATIONS

Nine space stations have orbited Earth. The former **Soviet Union** launched six space stations in the 1970s. All were named *Salyut*.

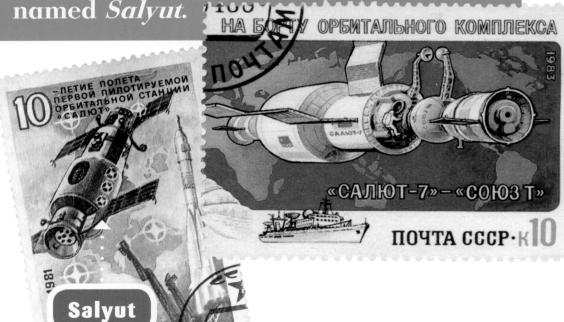

Salyut

Skylab

The United States launched *Skylab* in 1973. This space station had a powerful **telescope**.

The Soviet Union started building *Mir* in 1986. They finished 10 years later. Spacecraft from other countries visited this space station.

Fifteen countries built the International Space Station. The first pieces went to space in 1998. Spacecraft delivered the **truss**, robot arms, and other parts. Crews made **space walks** to put the parts together.

DID YOU KNOW?

The ISS is the most expensive object ever built. It cost more than $100 billion.

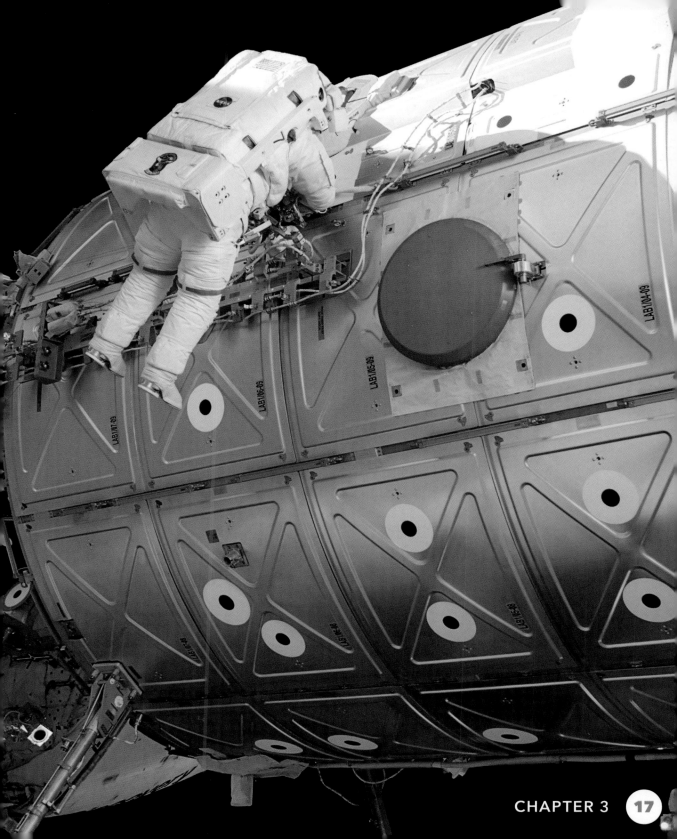

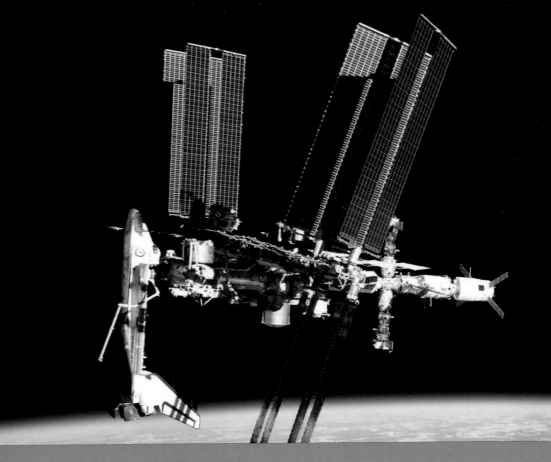

The ISS is huge. It is the size of a football field. It has the living space of a five-bedroom house!

The space station weighs about a million pounds (450,000 kilograms). Its weight makes it fall as it orbits. Small engines push the space station back up. It orbits Earth every 90 minutes.

TAKE A LOOK!

The ISS is made up of 14 modules where crew live and work. They are attached to the main truss. The truss supports the solar panels and other equipment.

① Solar Panels
② Crew Modules
③ Main Truss
④ Heat Radiators

Crews have lived on the ISS since 2000. Their work helps people get ready to explore other planets. Someday a spacecraft might carry people from the space station to Mars!

ACTIVITIES & TOOLS

The International Space Station can be seen at night with the naked eye. When will it pass over your home? Go to:

https://spotthestation.nasa.gov/sightings/

Enter in your country, state or region, and city. Then go outside at the designated time and look up!

What should you look for?

The space station looks like an airplane or a very bright star moving across the sky, except it doesn't have flashing lights or change direction. It will also be moving quite a bit faster than a typical airplane. That's because airplanes fly at about 600 miles per hour (966 km per hour), whereas the space station travels at 17,500 miles per hour (28,160 km per hour).

GLOSSARY

astronauts: People who have been trained to fly aboard a spacecraft and work in space.

docking port: A place where a spacecraft can connect with a space station; doorways called hatches join together to make a tunnel between the spacecraft and space station.

launch: To send a spacecraft into space.

modules: Parts of a space station.

orbit: To travel around the sun or other object in space.

satellite: An object that circles another body in space.

solar panels: Groups of solar cells; solar cells collect energy from the sun to make electricity.

Soviet Union: A large country in eastern Europe and western Asia that broke apart in 1991; Russia was once part of the Soviet Union and now runs its space program.

space walks: To leave a spacecraft and move around in space; astronauts wear space suits when they make space walks.

spacecraft: A vehicle that travels in space.

telescope: A tool that makes faraway objects look larger and nearer; large telescopes can see deep into space.

truss: A long, thick beam; a truss holds the parts of the International Space Station together.

INDEX

TO LEARN MORE

Learning more is as easy as 1, 2, 3.

1) **Go to www.factsurfer.com**

2) **Enter "spacestations" into the search box.**

3) **Click the "Surf" button to see a list of websites.**

With factsurfer, finding more information is just a click away.